70 Bartending and Cocktails Recipes for Home

By: Kelly Johnson

Table of Contents

Classic Cocktails:
- Martini
- Margarita
- Old Fashioned
- Negroni
- Moscow Mule
- Manhattan

Tropical and Fruity Cocktails:
- Piña Colada
- Mai Tai
- Sex on the Beach
- Bahama Mama

Summer Cocktails:
- Gin and Tonic
- Mint Julep
- Paloma
- Aperol Spritz
- Tom Collins

Unique and Craft Cocktails:
- Blackberry Smash
- Cucumber Basil Gimlet
- Rosemary Greyhound

Sparkling Cocktails:
- French 75
- Bellini
- Kir Royale
- Sparkling Mojito
- Elderflower Sparkler

Herb-Infused Cocktails:
- Basil Smash
- Thyme and Honey Whiskey Sour
- Cilantro Jalapeño Margarita
- Rosemary Vodka Lemonade
- Mint Chocolate Martini

Tequila-Based Cocktails:
- Tequila Sunrise

- Blood Orange Margarita
- Spicy Pineapple Cilantro Margarita
- Cucumber Jalapeño Tequila Cooler
- Smoky Mezcal Paloma

Whiskey and Bourbon Cocktails:
- Whiskey Sour
- Boulevardier
- Maple Bourbon Smash
- Black Manhattan
- Irish Coffee

Vodka Cocktails:
- Cosmopolitan
- Lemon Drop Martini
- Espresso Martini
- Cranberry Mule
- Watermelon Vodka Lemonade

Rum Cocktails:
- Daiquiri
- Rum Punch
- Coconut Mojito
- Dark and Stormy
- Pineapple Rum Slush

Gin Cocktails:
- Gimlet
- Aviation
- Southside
- Rosemary Gin Fizz

Champagne Cocktails:
- Classic Champagne Cocktail
- Hugo
- Black Velvet
- Bramble Royale

Non-Alcoholic Mocktails:
- Virgin Mojito
- Shirley Temple
- Cucumber Mint Cooler
- Berry Sparkler

Seasonal and Holiday Cocktails:
- Apple Cider Bourbon Smash
- Cranberry Orange Mimosa

- Pumpkin Spice White Russian
- Eggnog Martini

Herb and Fruit Infusions:
- Infused Berry Vodka
- Citrus Basil Gin
- Cucumber Mint Tequila
- Rosemary Infused Bourbon

Coffee and Dessert Cocktails:
- White Russian
- Chocolate Martini

Classic Cocktails:
Martini

Ingredients:

- 2 1/2 ounces (75 ml) gin
- 1/2 ounce (15 ml) dry vermouth
- Ice cubes
- Lemon twist or olive, for garnish

Instructions:

Chill the glass: Place your Martini glass in the freezer or fill it with ice water to chill while you prepare the cocktail.

Prepare the mixing glass: Fill a mixing glass with ice cubes to chill the ingredients.

Add gin and vermouth: Pour the gin and dry vermouth into the mixing glass over the ice.

Stir or shake: Some people prefer their Martinis stirred to maintain a silky texture, while others prefer them shaken for a slightly cloudy appearance and aeration. Stirring is the traditional method. If you choose to shake, do it quickly and strain the mixture into the glass.

Strain into the glass: Discard the ice from the chilled Martini glass and strain the mixed ingredients from the mixing glass into the glass.

Garnish: Twist a lemon peel over the drink to release its oils, or add an olive as a garnish. You can also choose to use a lemon twist and drop it into the drink.

Enjoy: Sip and savor the classic Martini!

Remember, the ratio of gin to vermouth can be adjusted to suit your personal taste preferences. Some people prefer a drier Martini with less vermouth, while others like a slightly wetter version with more vermouth. Feel free to experiment and find the perfect balance for you. Cheers!

Margarita

Ingredients:

- 2 ounces (60 ml) tequila
- 1 ounce (30 ml) triple sec or orange liqueur
- 3/4 ounce (22.5 ml) freshly squeezed lime juice
- Ice cubes
- Salt (for rimming the glass)
- Lime wedge (for garnish)

Instructions:

Rim the glass: Begin by rimming the edge of a glass with salt. To do this, moisten the rim with a lime wedge, then dip it into salt spread on a plate. This step is optional and can be skipped if you prefer your Margarita without a salted rim.
Mix the ingredients: In a shaker, combine the tequila, triple sec, and freshly squeezed lime juice.
Shake or stir: Fill the shaker with ice cubes and shake well for about 15-20 seconds to chill the ingredients. Alternatively, you can stir the ingredients in a mixing glass if you prefer.
Strain into the glass: Strain the mixed ingredients into the prepared glass over ice.
Garnish: Garnish the drink with a lime wedge on the rim of the glass.
Serve and enjoy: Your classic Margarita is ready to be enjoyed! Adjust the ingredients to suit your taste preferences.

If you like variations, you can try adding different fruits like strawberry or mango for flavored Margaritas. Additionally, you can experiment with different types of tequila to find your preferred flavor profile. Cheers!

Old Fashioned

Ingredients:

- 2 oz (60 ml) bourbon or rye whiskey
- 1 sugar cube (or 1/2 oz simple syrup)
- 2-3 dashes Angostura bitters
- Orange twist (for garnish)
- Ice cubes

Instructions:

Start with the sugar: If using a sugar cube, place it in an Old Fashioned glass. If you prefer simple syrup, you can add 1/2 oz directly to the glass.
Add bitters: Add 2-3 dashes of Angostura bitters to the sugar in the glass.
Muddle: Using a muddler or the back of a spoon, muddle the sugar and bitters together to dissolve the sugar and create a paste.
Add whiskey: Pour the bourbon or rye whiskey over the sugar and bitters mixture.
Ice: Add a few ice cubes to the glass. You can use a large ice cube or several smaller ones.
Stir: Stir the ingredients in the glass gently to chill the drink. Some people prefer stirring for a longer period to dilute the drink slightly, but it's a matter of personal preference.
Garnish: Express the oil from an orange twist over the drink by holding it over the glass and giving it a twist, then drop it into the glass as a garnish.
Enjoy: Sip and savor the classic and sophisticated taste of an Old Fashioned.

Remember, the Old Fashioned is a versatile cocktail, and you can adjust the sweetness and bitterness to your liking. Some people also like to experiment with different types of bitters or garnishes. Feel free to make it your own!

Negroni

Ingredients:

- 1 oz (30 ml) gin
- 1 oz (30 ml) sweet vermouth
- 1 oz (30 ml) Campari
- Orange slice or twist (for garnish)
- Ice cubes

Instructions:

Fill a mixing glass with ice cubes.
Add the ingredients: Pour the gin, sweet vermouth, and Campari over the ice in the mixing glass.
Stir: Stir the ingredients well to chill the mixture. Some variations of the Negroni involve shaking, but the classic method is to stir.
Strain: Strain the mixture into a rocks glass filled with ice.
Garnish: Garnish the drink with an orange slice or twist. You can express the oils from the orange peel over the drink by giving it a twist before dropping it into the glass.
Enjoy: Sip and enjoy the distinctive flavors of the Negroni.

The Negroni is known for its equal parts of gin, sweet vermouth, and Campari, creating a harmonious blend of botanicals, sweetness, and bitterness. If you find the classic Negroni a bit too bitter, you can adjust the proportions to suit your taste. Some people also enjoy experimenting with different gins or vermouths to create their own variations of this iconic cocktail. Cheers!

Moscow Mule

Ingredients:

- 2 oz (60 ml) vodka
- 4 oz (120 ml) ginger beer
- 1/2 oz (15 ml) fresh lime juice
- Ice cubes
- Lime wheel or wedge (for garnish)
- Mint sprig (optional, for garnish)

Instructions:

Fill a copper mug (or a highball glass) with ice cubes.
Pour the vodka over the ice in the mug.
Add fresh lime juice: Squeeze the juice from half a lime (about 1/2 oz) into the mug.
Top with ginger beer: Pour the ginger beer over the vodka and lime juice. You can adjust the amount of ginger beer to your taste preferences.
Stir gently: Use a stirring stick or spoon to gently mix the ingredients together.
Garnish: Garnish the drink with a lime wheel or wedge on the rim of the mug. Optionally, add a sprig of mint for extra freshness.
Enjoy: Sip and savor the zesty and effervescent flavors of the Moscow Mule!

The Moscow Mule is known for its distinctive presentation in a copper mug, which not only adds a touch of style but also helps keep the drink colder. Feel free to customize the recipe to suit your taste by adjusting the proportions of vodka, ginger beer, and lime juice. Cheers!

Manhattan

Ingredients:

- 2 oz (60 ml) rye whiskey or bourbon
- 1 oz (30 ml) sweet vermouth
- 2-3 dashes Angostura bitters
- Maraschino cherry (for garnish)
- Orange twist (optional, for garnish)
- Ice cubes

Instructions:

Fill a mixing glass with ice cubes.
Add the ingredients: Pour the rye whiskey (or bourbon), sweet vermouth, and Angostura bitters into the mixing glass.
Stir: Stir the ingredients well in the mixing glass to chill the mixture. Some variations involve shaking, but stirring is the traditional method.
Strain: Strain the mixture into a chilled cocktail glass.
Garnish: Garnish the drink with a maraschino cherry. Optionally, you can express the oil from an orange twist over the drink by giving it a twist and then dropping it into the glass.
Enjoy: Sip and savor the sophisticated and balanced flavors of the Manhattan.

The choice between rye whiskey and bourbon can be a matter of personal preference. Rye whiskey is often preferred for its spicier and drier profile, while bourbon adds a bit of sweetness. Feel free to experiment and find the combination that suits your taste. Adjust the level of sweetness by varying the amount of vermouth or by using a different brand of vermouth. Cheers!

Tropical and Fruity Cocktails:
Piña Colada

Ingredients:

- 2 oz white rum
- 3 oz pineapple juice
- 1 oz coconut cream
- Pineapple slices and maraschino cherries for garnish
- Ice cubes

Instructions:

In a blender, combine the white rum, pineapple juice, coconut cream, and a handful of ice cubes.
Blend until the mixture is smooth and creamy.
Pour the Piña Colada into a chilled glass.
Garnish with a pineapple slice and a maraschino cherry.
Optional: You can also garnish the rim of the glass with shredded coconut for added flair.

Feel free to adjust the ingredient quantities based on your taste preferences. Some variations include adding a splash of lime juice for extra acidity or using different types of rum for unique flavor profiles. Enjoy responsibly!

Mai Tai

Ingredients:

- 2 oz white rum
- 1 oz dark rum
- 3/4 oz lime juice (freshly squeezed)
- 1/2 oz orange liqueur (such as triple sec or orange curaçao)
- 1/2 oz orgeat syrup
- Ice cubes
- Mint sprig and lime wheel for garnish

Instructions:

Fill a shaker with ice cubes.
Add the white rum, dark rum, lime juice, orange liqueur, and orgeat syrup to the shaker.
Shake the ingredients well to chill the mixture.
Strain the cocktail into an old-fashioned glass filled with crushed ice.
Garnish with a mint sprig and a lime wheel.
Optionally, you can also float a bit of dark rum on top by gently pouring it over the back of a spoon to create a layered effect.

Keep in mind that there are many variations of the Mai Tai, and different bartenders may have their own interpretations. Some recipes might include pineapple juice or other ingredients. Adjust the proportions to suit your taste preferences, and enjoy this classic cocktail responsibly!

Sex on the Beach

Ingredients:

- 1 1/2 oz vodka
- 1/2 oz peach schnapps
- 2 oz cranberry juice
- 2 oz orange juice
- Ice cubes
- Orange slice and maraschino cherry for garnish

Instructions:

Fill a shaker with ice cubes.
Add vodka, peach schnapps, cranberry juice, and orange juice to the shaker.
Shake the ingredients well to combine and chill the mixture.
Strain the cocktail into a highball glass filled with ice.
Garnish with an orange slice and a maraschino cherry.

Keep in mind that variations of this cocktail exist, and some may include different fruit juices or additional ingredients. Additionally, the garnishes can be adjusted based on personal preference. It's a fun and vibrant drink that's often associated with beach-themed parties and tropical settings. Enjoy responsibly!

Bahama Mama

Ingredients:

- 1 1/2 oz dark rum
- 1/2 oz coconut rum
- 1/2 oz banana liqueur
- 1/2 oz grenadine
- 1 oz orange juice
- 1 oz pineapple juice
- Crushed ice
- Orange slice and cherry for garnish

Instructions:

Fill a shaker with crushed ice.
Add dark rum, coconut rum, banana liqueur, grenadine, orange juice, and pineapple juice to the shaker.
Shake well to combine and chill the mixture.
Strain the cocktail into a highball glass filled with ice.
Garnish with an orange slice and a cherry.

The Bahama Mama is known for its sweet and tropical flavors, making it a popular choice for beachside enjoyment. Keep in mind that there are variations of this cocktail, and you may find recipes with slightly different ingredient proportions. Adjustments can be made based on personal preference. Enjoy responsibly!

Summer Cocktails:
Gin and Tonic

Ingredients:

- 2 oz gin
- Tonic water
- Ice cubes
- Lime wedge or slice for garnish

Instructions:

Fill a highball glass with ice cubes.
Pour 2 ounces of gin over the ice.
Top up the glass with tonic water.
Stir gently to mix the ingredients.
Garnish with a lime wedge or slice.

Feel free to adjust the gin-to-tonic ratio based on your personal preference for a stronger or lighter drink. You can also experiment with different types of gin to explore various flavor profiles. The Gin and Tonic is a versatile cocktail enjoyed for its simplicity and the ability to customize it to suit individual tastes. Enjoy responsibly!

Mint Julep

Ingredients:

- 2 1/2 oz bourbon
- 8-10 fresh mint leaves, plus a sprig for garnish
- 1/2 oz simple syrup (or more, to taste)
- Crushed ice

Instructions:

In a glass or silver cup, muddle the fresh mint leaves and simple syrup together to release the mint's flavor.
Fill the glass with crushed ice.
Pour the bourbon over the ice and mint mixture.
Stir gently to combine and frost the glass.
Garnish with a mint sprig.

It's essential to use fresh, high-quality mint for the best flavor. The crushed ice helps to chill the drink and contributes to the signature frosty appearance of the Mint Julep. Adjust the amount of simple syrup based on your sweetness preference, and choose a bourbon that you enjoy. This cocktail is not only delicious but also a classic symbol of Southern hospitality. Enjoy responsibly!

Paloma

Ingredients:

- 2 oz tequila (blanco or reposado)
- 1/2 oz lime juice (freshly squeezed)
- Grapefruit soda
- Ice cubes
- Grapefruit wedge or slice for garnish
- Salt for rimming the glass (optional)

Instructions:

If desired, rim a highball glass with salt. To do this, moisten the rim of the glass with a lime wedge, then dip it into salt.
Fill the glass with ice cubes.
In a shaker, combine the tequila and freshly squeezed lime juice.
Shake well to mix and chill the ingredients.
Strain the tequila and lime juice mixture into the prepared glass over ice.
Top up the glass with grapefruit soda. You can adjust the amount based on your taste preference.
Stir gently to combine.
Garnish with a grapefruit wedge or slice.

The Paloma is a versatile cocktail, and you can experiment with different types of grapefruit soda or add a splash of club soda for a bit of effervescence. It's a delightful and easy-to-make drink that's perfect for warm weather or any time you're in the mood for a refreshing cocktail. Enjoy responsibly!

Aperol Spritz

Ingredients:

- 2 oz Aperol
- 3 oz Prosecco (or any other sparkling wine)
- Splash of club soda
- Orange slice for garnish
- Ice cubes

Instructions:

Fill a wine glass or a large balloon glass with ice cubes.
Pour 2 ounces of Aperol over the ice.
Add 3 ounces of Prosecco to the glass.
Top it off with a splash of club soda.
Gently stir the ingredients to combine.
Garnish with an orange slice.

The Aperol Spritz is known for its bittersweet and citrusy flavors, making it a popular choice for aperitivo hour. Adjust the proportions to your liking, as some people prefer a slightly stronger or lighter version. It's a light and effervescent cocktail that's perfect for warm weather or as a pre-dinner drink. Enjoy this classic Italian aperitif responsibly!

Tom Collins

Ingredients:

- 2 oz gin
- 1 oz simple syrup
- 3/4 oz fresh lemon juice
- Club soda
- Ice cubes
- Lemon slice and cherry for garnish

Instructions:

Fill a Collins glass with ice cubes.
In a shaker, combine the gin, simple syrup, and fresh lemon juice.
Shake well to mix and chill the ingredients.
Strain the mixture into the Collins glass over ice.
Top up the glass with club soda.
Stir gently to combine.
Garnish with a lemon slice and a cherry.

The Tom Collins is known for its effervescence and balanced sweet-tart flavor. Adjust the amount of simple syrup and lemon juice based on your taste preferences. It's a timeless cocktail that's easy to make and perfect for sipping on a warm day. Enjoy responsibly!

Unique and Craft Cocktails:
Blackberry Smash

Ingredients:

- 2 oz bourbon
- 1/2 oz simple syrup
- 1/2 oz freshly squeezed lemon juice
- 8-10 fresh blackberries
- Mint leaves (optional, for garnish)
- Ice cubes

Instructions:

In a mixing glass, muddle the fresh blackberries with simple syrup and freshly squeezed lemon juice.
Add bourbon to the mixing glass.
Fill the glass with ice and shake the ingredients well to combine and chill the mixture.
Strain the mixture into a rocks glass filled with ice.
Garnish with fresh mint leaves if desired.
Optionally, you can add a few whole blackberries to the glass for an extra burst of flavor and a visually appealing touch.

The Blackberry Smash offers a perfect balance of sweetness, tartness, and the rich flavor of bourbon. It's a great cocktail for those who enjoy fruity and refreshing drinks with a hint of complexity. Enjoy responsibly!

Cucumber Basil Gimlet

Ingredients:

- 2 oz gin
- 3/4 oz simple syrup
- 3/4 oz freshly squeezed lime juice
- 4-5 slices of cucumber
- 4-6 fresh basil leaves
- Ice cubes

Instructions:

In a shaker, muddle the cucumber slices and basil leaves to release their flavors.
Add gin, simple syrup, and freshly squeezed lime juice to the shaker.
Fill the shaker with ice cubes.
Shake the ingredients well to combine and chill the mixture.
Strain the mixture into a chilled martini or rocks glass.
Optionally, garnish with a cucumber wheel or basil leaf.

This Cucumber Basil Gimlet offers a delightful combination of botanical and herbal notes, making it a perfect choice for those who enjoy a light and aromatic cocktail. Adjust the simple syrup quantity to achieve your preferred level of sweetness. Enjoy this refreshing drink responsibly!

Rosemary Greyhound

Ingredients:

- 2 oz vodka or gin
- 4 oz fresh grapefruit juice
- 1/2 oz rosemary simple syrup (see instructions below)
- Rosemary sprig for garnish
- Ice cubes

For Rosemary Simple Syrup:

- 1/2 cup water
- 1/2 cup granulated sugar
- 3-4 fresh rosemary sprigs

Instructions:

Rosemary Simple Syrup:

In a small saucepan, combine water, sugar, and rosemary sprigs.
Bring the mixture to a simmer over medium heat, stirring until the sugar dissolves.
Let it simmer for a few minutes to infuse the rosemary flavor.
Remove from heat and let it cool completely.
Strain the syrup to remove the rosemary sprigs, and store it in a sealed container in the refrigerator until ready to use.

Rosemary Greyhound:

In a shaker, combine vodka or gin, fresh grapefruit juice, and rosemary simple syrup.
Fill the shaker with ice cubes.
Shake the ingredients well to combine and chill the mixture.
Strain the mixture into a rocks glass filled with ice.
Garnish with a sprig of fresh rosemary.

The Rosemary Greyhound adds an herbal and aromatic element to the classic citrusy and refreshing Greyhound. Adjust the rosemary simple syrup to your preferred sweetness level. Enjoy responsibly!

Sparkling Cocktails
French 75

Ingredients:

- 1 1/2 oz gin
- 3/4 oz fresh lemon juice
- 1/2 oz simple syrup
- Champagne or sparkling wine
- Lemon twist or cherry for garnish
- Ice cubes

Instructions:

In a shaker, combine gin, fresh lemon juice, and simple syrup.
Fill the shaker with ice cubes.
Shake the ingredients well to combine and chill the mixture.
Strain the mixture into a chilled champagne flute or a Collins glass filled with ice.
Top it off with champagne or sparkling wine.
Gently stir to combine.
Garnish with a lemon twist or a cherry.

The French 75 is known for its elegance and balance, with the effervescence of the champagne complementing the citrusy and botanical flavors from the gin and lemon. Adjust the simple syrup quantity to your preferred sweetness level. This cocktail is a classic choice for celebrations or any occasion where you want a bubbly and sophisticated drink. Enjoy responsibly!

Bellini

Ingredients:

- 1 1/2 oz gin
- 3/4 oz fresh lemon juice
- 1/2 oz simple syrup
- Champagne or sparkling wine
- Lemon twist or cherry for garnish
- Ice cubes

Instructions:

In a shaker, combine gin, fresh lemon juice, and simple syrup.
Fill the shaker with ice cubes.
Shake the ingredients well to combine and chill the mixture.
Strain the mixture into a chilled champagne flute or a Collins glass filled with ice.
Top it off with champagne or sparkling wine.
Gently stir to combine.
Garnish with a lemon twist or a cherry.

The French 75 is known for its elegance and balance, with the effervescence of the champagne complementing the citrusy and botanical flavors from the gin and lemon. Adjust the simple syrup quantity to your preferred sweetness level. This cocktail is a classic choice for celebrations or any occasion where you want a bubbly and sophisticated drink. Enjoy responsibly!

Kir Royale

Ingredients:

- 1/2 oz crème de cassis (blackcurrant liqueur)
- Champagne or sparkling wine
- Lemon twist or blackcurrant for garnish (optional)

Instructions:

Chill a Champagne flute in the refrigerator or freezer.
Pour the crème de cassis into the chilled flute.
Top up the glass with Champagne or sparkling wine.
Gently stir to mix the ingredients.
Optionally, garnish with a lemon twist or a blackcurrant.

The Kir Royale is known for its simple preparation and delightful flavor profile. The blackcurrant liqueur adds a touch of sweetness and a deep, rich color to the Champagne. Adjust the ratio of crème de cassis to Champagne based on your taste preferences. This cocktail is a classic choice for toasting and celebrating special moments. Enjoy responsibly!

Sparkling Mojito

Ingredients:

- 2 oz white rum
- 1 oz fresh lime juice
- 2 teaspoons sugar (adjust to taste)
- 6-8 fresh mint leaves
- Sparkling water or club soda
- Ice cubes
- Lime wedge and mint sprig for garnish

Instructions:

In a glass, muddle the fresh mint leaves with sugar and fresh lime juice. Muddle just enough to release the mint flavor without tearing the leaves.
Add white rum to the glass.
Fill the glass with ice cubes.
Top up the glass with sparkling water or club soda.
Stir gently to mix the ingredients.
Garnish with a lime wedge and a sprig of fresh mint.
Optionally, you can add more sugar or lime juice to adjust the sweetness and tartness to your liking.

The Sparkling Mojito combines the classic flavors of a Mojito with the effervescence of sparkling water, creating a light and bubbly cocktail that's perfect for warm weather or any occasion. Enjoy this refreshing drink responsibly!

Elderflower Sparkler

Ingredients:

- 1 oz elderflower liqueur (such as St-Germain)
- 4 oz sparkling wine (Prosecco, Champagne, or other sparkling wine)
- Ice cubes
- Lemon twist or edible flowers for garnish (optional)

Instructions:

Chill a flute or wine glass.
Pour the elderflower liqueur into the chilled glass.
Top it up with sparkling wine.
Add ice cubes if desired.
Gently stir to combine the ingredients.
Optionally, garnish with a lemon twist or edible flowers.

The Elderflower Sparkler is known for its delicate and floral notes, making it a sophisticated and refreshing choice for various occasions. The elderflower liqueur adds a subtle sweetness and floral aroma to the bubbly effervescence of the sparkling wine. Adjust the elderflower liqueur quantity based on your taste preferences. Enjoy this elegant cocktail responsibly!

Herb-Infused Cocktails:
Basil Smash

Ingredients:

- 2 oz gin
- 3/4 oz fresh lemon juice
- 1/2 oz simple syrup
- Fresh basil leaves (about 8-10 leaves)
- Ice cubes

Instructions:

In a shaker, muddle the fresh basil leaves with the simple syrup to release their flavors.
Add gin and fresh lemon juice to the shaker.
Fill the shaker with ice cubes.
Shake the ingredients well to combine and chill the mixture.
Strain the mixture into a rocks glass filled with ice.
Optionally, you can double-strain the cocktail to remove the basil bits for a smoother texture.
Garnish with a fresh basil leaf.

The Basil Smash is known for its bright and aromatic qualities, with the basil adding a unique herbal note to the classic gin and citrus combination. Adjust the simple syrup quantity based on your preferred level of sweetness. It's a refreshing and well-balanced cocktail that's perfect for warm weather or any time you're in the mood for a flavorful and herb-infused drink. Enjoy responsibly!

Thyme and Honey Whiskey Sour

Ingredients:

- 2 oz bourbon or whiskey
- 3/4 oz fresh lemon juice
- 1/2 oz honey syrup (1:1 ratio of honey to water)
- Fresh thyme sprigs
- Ice cubes

Instructions:

To make the honey syrup, combine equal parts honey and water in a saucepan over low heat. Stir until the honey dissolves. Let it cool before using.
In a shaker, muddle a couple of thyme sprigs with the honey syrup to release the thyme flavor.
Add bourbon or whiskey and fresh lemon juice to the shaker.
Fill the shaker with ice cubes.
Shake the ingredients well to combine and chill the mixture.
Strain the mixture into a rocks glass filled with ice.
Optionally, garnish with a thyme sprig.

The Thyme and Honey Whiskey Sour introduces herbal and sweet elements to the classic sour profile, creating a well-balanced and aromatic cocktail. Adjust the honey syrup quantity based on your sweetness preference. Enjoy this flavorful twist on a timeless classic responsibly!

Cilantro Jalapeño Margarita

Ingredients:

- 2 oz tequila (silver or blanco)
- 1 oz triple sec or orange liqueur
- 1 oz fresh lime juice
- 1/2 oz agave syrup or simple syrup (adjust to taste)
- 2-3 slices of fresh jalapeño
- Fresh cilantro leaves
- Ice cubes
- Salt or chili salt for rimming the glass (optional)
- Lime wedge or wheel for garnish

Instructions:

If desired, rim a rocks glass with salt or chili salt by moistening the rim with a lime wedge and dipping it into the salt.
In a shaker, muddle the fresh jalapeño slices with cilantro leaves. Adjust the amount of jalapeño based on your spice preference.
Add tequila, triple sec, fresh lime juice, and agave syrup to the shaker.
Fill the shaker with ice cubes.
Shake the ingredients well to infuse the flavors and chill the mixture.
Strain the mixture into the prepared glass over ice.
Garnish with a lime wedge or wheel.

The Cilantro Jalapeño Margarita offers a bold and refreshing twist on the classic Margarita, with the herbal and spicy elements enhancing the overall flavor profile. Adjust the sweetness level by modifying the amount of agave syrup. Enjoy this zesty and flavorful cocktail responsibly!

Rosemary Vodka Lemonade

Ingredients:

- 2 oz vodka
- 4 oz fresh lemonade
- 1/2 oz simple syrup (optional, adjust to taste)
- 1 sprig of fresh rosemary
- Ice cubes
- Lemon slice for garnish

Instructions:

In a shaker, add vodka and fresh lemonade.
If desired, add simple syrup to sweeten the mixture. Adjust the sweetness level to your preference.
Take a sprig of fresh rosemary and gently clap it between your hands to release its aromatic oils. Add it to the shaker.
Fill the shaker with ice cubes.
Shake the ingredients well to infuse the rosemary flavor and chill the mixture.
Strain the mixture into a glass filled with ice.
Garnish with a lemon slice and an additional sprig of fresh rosemary.

The Rosemary Vodka Lemonade offers a refreshing and herbal twist on the classic vodka lemonade. The rosemary adds a fragrant and earthy note to the drink, enhancing its overall appeal. Adjust the simple syrup quantity based on your sweetness preference. Enjoy this flavorful and aromatic cocktail responsibly!

Mint Chocolate Martini

Ingredients:

- 2 oz chocolate liqueur
- 1 oz vodka
- 1/2 oz crème de menthe (green or white)
- 1 oz cream or half-and-half
- Ice cubes
- Chocolate shavings or cocoa powder for garnish (optional)
- Mint sprig for garnish

Instructions:

In a shaker, add chocolate liqueur, vodka, crème de menthe, and cream.
Fill the shaker with ice cubes.
Shake the ingredients vigorously to chill the mixture.
Strain the mixture into a chilled martini glass.
Optionally, garnish with chocolate shavings or a sprinkle of cocoa powder on top.
Add a mint sprig for a fresh and aromatic touch.

The Mint Chocolate Martini is a delightful treat for those who enjoy the combination of chocolate and mint. Adjust the proportions based on your taste preferences. This cocktail is perfect for dessert or as a festive drink for special occasions. Enjoy responsibly!

Tequila-Based Cocktails:
Tequila Sunrise

Ingredients:

- 2 oz tequila
- 4 oz orange juice
- 1/2 oz grenadine
- Ice cubes
- Orange slice and maraschino cherry for garnish

Instructions:

Fill a highball glass with ice cubes.
Pour the tequila and orange juice into the glass.
Stir gently to mix the tequila and orange juice.
Slowly pour the grenadine over the back of a spoon or by drizzling it down the side of the glass, allowing it to settle at the bottom.
Let the grenadine settle, creating the distinct sunrise effect.
Garnish with an orange slice and a maraschino cherry.

Remember not to stir the drink too much after adding the grenadine to maintain the layered appearance. The Tequila Sunrise is known for its vibrant colors and sweet, fruity taste. Enjoy this classic cocktail responsibly!

Blood Orange Margarita

Ingredients:

- 2 oz tequila (silver or reposado)
- 1 oz triple sec or orange liqueur
- 1 oz fresh lime juice
- 2 oz fresh blood orange juice
- 1/2 oz agave syrup or simple syrup (adjust to taste)
- Salt or chili salt for rimming the glass (optional)
- Blood orange slice for garnish
- Ice cubes

Instructions:

If desired, rim a margarita glass with salt or chili salt by moistening the rim with a lime wedge and dipping it into the salt.
In a shaker, combine tequila, triple sec, fresh lime juice, fresh blood orange juice, and agave syrup.
Fill the shaker with ice cubes.
Shake the ingredients well to combine and chill the mixture.
Strain the mixture into the prepared glass over ice.
Garnish with a blood orange slice.

The Blood Orange Margarita offers a sweet and tart flavor with the distinctive taste of blood oranges, creating a visually appealing and delicious cocktail. Adjust the agave syrup quantity based on your sweetness preference. Enjoy this refreshing and colorful drink responsibly!

Spicy Pineapple Cilantro Margarita

Ingredients:

- 2 oz tequila (silver or reposado)
- 1 oz triple sec or orange liqueur
- 1 oz fresh lime juice
- 1 oz fresh pineapple juice
- 1/2 oz agave syrup or simple syrup (adjust to taste)
- 2-3 slices of fresh jalapeño (adjust to desired spice level)
- Fresh cilantro leaves
- Salt or chili salt for rimming the glass (optional)
- Pineapple wedge or cilantro sprig for garnish
- Ice cubes

Instructions:

If desired, rim a margarita glass with salt or chili salt by moistening the rim with a lime wedge and dipping it into the salt.
In a shaker, muddle the fresh cilantro leaves and jalapeño slices with agave syrup.
Add tequila, triple sec, fresh lime juice, and fresh pineapple juice to the shaker.
Fill the shaker with ice cubes.
Shake the ingredients well to combine, infuse the flavors, and chill the mixture.
Strain the mixture into the prepared glass over ice.
Garnish with a pineapple wedge or cilantro sprig.

The Spicy Pineapple Cilantro Margarita offers a balance of sweetness, tartness, herbal freshness, and a touch of heat. Adjust the agave syrup and jalapeño quantity based on your taste preferences. Enjoy this flavorful and zesty cocktail responsibly!

Cucumber Jalapeño Tequila Cooler

Ingredients:

- 2 oz tequila (silver or reposado)
- 1 oz triple sec or orange liqueur
- 1 oz fresh lime juice
- 4-5 slices of cucumber
- 2-3 slices of jalapeño (adjust to desired spice level)
- 1/2 oz agave syrup or simple syrup (adjust to taste)
- Mint leaves for muddling and garnish
- Soda water or club soda
- Ice cubes

Instructions:

In a shaker, muddle the cucumber slices, jalapeño slices, and mint leaves with agave syrup.
Add tequila, triple sec, and fresh lime juice to the shaker.
Fill the shaker with ice cubes.
Shake the ingredients well to combine, infuse the flavors, and chill the mixture.
Strain the mixture into a glass filled with ice.
Top it up with soda water or club soda.
Garnish with a mint sprig.

The Cucumber Jalapeño Tequila Cooler offers a unique combination of refreshing cucumber, spicy jalapeño, and the smoothness of tequila. Adjust the agave syrup and jalapeño slices based on your taste preferences. Enjoy this invigorating and spicy cocktail responsibly!

Smoky Mezcal Paloma

Ingredients:

- 2 oz mezcal
- 3 oz grapefruit soda
- 1 oz fresh lime juice
- 1/2 oz agave syrup or simple syrup (adjust to taste)
- Salt for rimming the glass (optional)
- Grapefruit wedge for garnish
- Ice cubes

Instructions:

If desired, rim a highball glass with salt by moistening the rim with a grapefruit wedge and dipping it into the salt.
In a shaker, combine mezcal, fresh lime juice, and agave syrup.
Fill the shaker with ice cubes.
Shake the ingredients well to combine and chill the mixture.
Strain the mixture into the prepared glass over ice.
Top it up with grapefruit soda.
Gently stir to combine.
Garnish with a grapefruit wedge.

The Smoky Mezcal Paloma is known for its bold and smoky flavor profile, thanks to the use of mezcal. Adjust the agave syrup quantity based on your sweetness preference. Enjoy this intriguing and smoky twist on the classic Paloma responsibly!

Whiskey and Bourbon Cocktails
Whiskey Sour

Ingredients:

- 2 oz whiskey (bourbon or rye)
- 3/4 oz fresh lemon juice
- 1/2 oz simple syrup
- Ice cubes
- Lemon slice or cherry for garnish (optional)

Instructions:

In a shaker, combine the whiskey, fresh lemon juice, and simple syrup.
Fill the shaker with ice cubes.
Shake the ingredients well to combine and chill the mixture.
Strain the mixture into a rocks glass filled with ice.
Optionally, garnish with a lemon slice or a cherry.

The Whiskey Sour is appreciated for its balanced sweet-tart flavor and the richness of the whiskey. You can adjust the proportions of lemon juice and simple syrup based on your taste preferences. Some variations also include an egg white for a frothier texture, but this is optional.

Enjoy this classic cocktail responsibly!

Boulevardier

Ingredients:

- 1 1/2 oz bourbon or rye whiskey
- 3/4 oz sweet vermouth
- 3/4 oz Campari
- Orange twist or cherry for garnish

Instructions:

Fill a mixing glass with ice.
Add bourbon or rye whiskey, sweet vermouth, and Campari to the glass.
Stir the ingredients well to chill the mixture.
Strain the mixture into a rocks glass filled with ice.
Optionally, garnish with an orange twist or a cherry.

The Boulevardier offers a complex flavor profile with the richness of the whiskey, the sweetness of the vermouth, and the bitter notes from Campari. Adjust the proportions based on your taste preferences. It's a sophisticated cocktail that's perfect for those who enjoy bold and bitter drinks. Enjoy responsibly!

Maple Bourbon Smash

Ingredients:

- 2 oz bourbon
- 1/2 oz pure maple syrup
- 3/4 oz fresh lemon juice
- 4-6 fresh mint leaves
- Orange slice for garnish
- Ice cubes

Instructions:

In a shaker, muddle the fresh mint leaves with the maple syrup and fresh lemon juice.
Add bourbon to the shaker.
Fill the shaker with ice cubes.
Shake the ingredients well to combine, muddle the mint, and chill the mixture.
Strain the mixture into a rocks glass filled with ice.
Garnish with an orange slice.

The Maple Bourbon Smash offers a delightful combination of rich bourbon, sweet maple syrup, and the bright citrusy kick from fresh lemon juice. The mint adds a refreshing herbal note to the drink. Adjust the maple syrup quantity based on your sweetness preference.

Enjoy this flavorful and well-balanced cocktail responsibly!

Irish Coffee

Ingredients:

- 1 1/2 oz Irish whiskey
- 6 oz hot brewed coffee
- 1 oz simple syrup (optional, to taste)
- Fresh whipped cream

Instructions:

Preheat a heat-resistant glass or mug by filling it with hot water. Let it sit for a minute, then discard the water.
Pour the hot brewed coffee into the preheated glass or mug.
Add the Irish whiskey to the coffee. If you prefer a sweeter taste, you can add simple syrup to taste.
Gently float a layer of fresh whipped cream on top of the coffee by pouring it over the back of a spoon. The cream should rest on the surface of the coffee.
Serve immediately and enjoy while the coffee is hot.

Irish Coffee is a classic and straightforward cocktail, known for its comforting warmth and rich flavors. Adjust the sweetness with simple syrup based on your preference, and savor the delightful combination of coffee, whiskey, and cream. Enjoy responsibly!

Vodka Cocktails
Cosmopolitan

Ingredients:

- 1 1/2 oz vodka
- 1 oz triple sec (orange liqueur)
- 1/2 oz cranberry juice
- 1/2 oz freshly squeezed lime juice
- Orange or lime twist for garnish
- Ice cubes

Instructions:

Fill a shaker with ice cubes.
Add vodka, triple sec, cranberry juice, and freshly squeezed lime juice to the shaker.
Shake the ingredients well to chill the mixture.
Strain the mixture into a chilled martini glass.
Garnish with an orange or lime twist.

The Cosmopolitan is known for its balance of sweet and tart flavors, with the cranberry juice providing a bright and fruity note. Adjust the quantities based on your personal taste preferences, and enjoy this classic cocktail in its stylish martini glass. Cheers!

Lemon Drop Martini

Ingredients:

- 2 oz vodka
- 3/4 oz triple sec (orange liqueur)
- 1 oz simple syrup
- 3/4 oz freshly squeezed lemon juice
- Lemon twist or sugared rim for garnish
- Ice cubes

Instructions:

Rim a chilled martini glass with sugar by moistening the rim with a lemon wedge and dipping it into sugar.
In a shaker, combine vodka, triple sec, simple syrup, and freshly squeezed lemon juice.
Fill the shaker with ice cubes.
Shake the ingredients well to combine and chill the mixture.
Strain the mixture into the prepared martini glass.
Garnish with a lemon twist.

The Lemon Drop Martini is known for its vibrant citrusy flavor and sweet undertones. Adjust the simple syrup quantity based on your sweetness preference. Some variations also use superfine sugar instead of simple syrup. It's a classic cocktail that's perfect for those who enjoy a crisp and tangy martini. Enjoy responsibly!

Espresso Martini

Ingredients:

- 1 1/2 oz vodka
- 1 oz coffee liqueur (such as Kahlúa)
- 1 oz freshly brewed espresso (cooled to room temperature)
- 1/2 oz simple syrup (optional, to taste)
- Ice cubes

Instructions:

Brew a shot of espresso and let it cool to room temperature.
In a shaker, combine vodka, coffee liqueur, and the freshly brewed and cooled espresso.
Add simple syrup to the shaker if you prefer a sweeter taste. Adjust the quantity based on your sweetness preference.
Fill the shaker with ice cubes.
Shake the ingredients well to combine and chill the mixture.
Strain the mixture into a chilled martini glass.
Optionally, you can garnish with coffee beans on top.

The Espresso Martini is known for its bold coffee flavor and smooth texture. It's a delightful after-dinner drink or a pick-me-up cocktail. Adjust the simple syrup quantity based on your taste preferences. Enjoy this sophisticated and caffeinated cocktail responsibly!

Cranberry Mule

Ingredients:

- 2 oz vodka
- 4 oz ginger beer
- 2 oz cranberry juice
- 1/2 oz fresh lime juice
- Cranberries and lime wedge for garnish
- Ice cubes

Instructions:

Fill a copper mug or glass with ice cubes.
Add vodka and fresh lime juice to the mug.
Pour in cranberry juice.
Top it off with ginger beer.
Stir gently to combine the ingredients.
Garnish with cranberries and a lime wedge.

The Cranberry Mule is known for its beautiful color and the perfect balance of sweet, tart, and spicy flavors. The ginger beer adds a refreshing kick, while the cranberry juice complements the overall taste. It's a fantastic choice for holiday gatherings or any time you want a vibrant and flavorful cocktail. Enjoy responsibly!

Watermelon Vodka Lemonade

Ingredients:

- 2 oz vodka
- 4 oz watermelon juice (freshly blended or store-bought)
- 2 oz fresh lemonade
- 1/2 oz simple syrup (optional, adjust to taste)
- Watermelon wedge or lemon wheel for garnish
- Ice cubes

Instructions:

In a shaker, combine vodka, watermelon juice, fresh lemonade, and simple syrup if desired.
Fill the shaker with ice cubes.
Shake the ingredients well to combine and chill the mixture.
Strain the mixture into a glass filled with ice.
Garnish with a watermelon wedge or a lemon wheel.

The Watermelon Vodka Lemonade offers a delightful blend of sweet watermelon, tart lemonade, and the crispness of vodka. Adjust the simple syrup quantity based on your sweetness preference. It's a perfect cocktail for warm weather or when you're in the mood for a light and fruity drink. Enjoy responsibly!

Rum Cocktails:
Daiquiri

Ingredients:

- 2 oz white rum
- 3/4 oz fresh lime juice
- 1/2 oz simple syrup
- Lime wheel or twist for garnish
- Ice cubes

Instructions:

Fill a shaker with ice cubes.
Add white rum, fresh lime juice, and simple syrup to the shaker.
Shake the ingredients well to combine and chill the mixture.
Strain the mixture into a chilled martini or coupe glass.
Garnish with a lime wheel or twist.

The Daiquiri is known for its bright and citrusy flavor, balanced with the sweetness of simple syrup and the smoothness of rum. It's a classic cocktail that can be easily customized by adjusting the sweetness level with simple syrup. Enjoy this timeless and refreshing drink responsibly!

Rum Punch

Ingredients:

- 2 oz light rum
- 1 oz dark rum
- 1 oz orange juice
- 1 oz pineapple juice
- 1/2 oz grenadine
- 1/2 oz fresh lime juice
- Orange slice and cherry for garnish
- Ice cubes

Instructions:

Fill a shaker with ice cubes.
Add light rum, dark rum, orange juice, pineapple juice, grenadine, and fresh lime juice to the shaker.
Shake the ingredients well to combine.
Strain the mixture into a glass filled with ice.
Garnish with an orange slice and a cherry.

The Rum Punch is known for its tropical and sweet taste, with the combination of citrus, pineapple, and grenadine providing a well-balanced flavor profile. Adjust the ingredients to your taste preferences and enjoy this fruity cocktail responsibly!

Coconut Mojito

Ingredients:

- 2 oz white rum
- 1 oz coconut cream or coconut milk
- 1 oz fresh lime juice
- 1 oz simple syrup
- 8-10 fresh mint leaves
- Soda water or club soda
- Lime wedge and mint sprig for garnish
- Ice cubes

Instructions:

In a glass, muddle the fresh mint leaves with simple syrup and fresh lime juice.
Add white rum and coconut cream to the glass.
Fill the glass with ice cubes.
Top it up with soda water or club soda.
Stir gently to combine the ingredients.
Garnish with a lime wedge and a sprig of fresh mint.

The Coconut Mojito offers a tropical and creamy twist to the classic Mojito, with the coconut cream adding richness and depth to the drink. Adjust the simple syrup quantity based on your sweetness preference. Enjoy this delightful and flavorful cocktail responsibly!

Dark and Stormy

Ingredients:

- 2 oz dark rum
- Ginger beer
- Lime wedge for garnish
- Ice cubes

Instructions:

Fill a highball glass with ice cubes.
Pour the dark rum over the ice.
Top it off with ginger beer, leaving some space at the top.
Stir gently to mix the ingredients.
Garnish with a lime wedge.

It's important to note that the traditional Dark and Stormy cocktail uses Gosling's Black Seal Rum. If you want to be authentic, using this specific dark rum is recommended. The layering of dark rum and ginger beer creates a visually appealing drink, and the combination of flavors is both bold and refreshing. Enjoy this classic cocktail responsibly!

Pineapple Rum Slush

Ingredients:

- 2 cups frozen pineapple chunks
- 2 oz white rum
- 1 oz coconut cream
- 1 oz pineapple juice
- 1/2 oz simple syrup (optional, to taste)
- Ice cubes
- Pineapple slice and mint sprig for garnish

Instructions:

In a blender, combine the frozen pineapple chunks, white rum, coconut cream, pineapple juice, and simple syrup if desired.
Blend the ingredients until smooth and slushy.
Taste and adjust the sweetness with more simple syrup if needed.
Pour the slush into a glass.
Garnish with a pineapple slice and a mint sprig.

The Pineapple Rum Slush is a refreshing and tropical cocktail, perfect for warm weather or as a delightful frozen treat. Adjust the simple syrup quantity based on your sweetness preference. Enjoy this frosty and flavorful drink responsibly!

Gin Cocktails:
Gimlet

Ingredients:

- 2 oz gin
- 3/4 oz fresh lime juice
- 1/2 oz simple syrup
- Lime wheel or twist for garnish
- Ice cubes

Instructions:

In a shaker, combine gin, fresh lime juice, and simple syrup.
Fill the shaker with ice cubes.
Shake the ingredients well to combine and chill the mixture.
Strain the mixture into a chilled martini or rocks glass.
Garnish with a lime wheel or twist.

The Gimlet is known for its simplicity and the perfect balance between the herbal notes of gin and the citrusy kick of lime. Adjust the simple syrup quantity based on your sweetness preference. It's a timeless cocktail that's easy to make and enjoyable year-round. Enjoy responsibly!

Aviation

Ingredients:

- 2 oz gin
- 1/2 oz maraschino liqueur
- 1/4 oz crème de violette
- 3/4 oz fresh lemon juice
- Maraschino cherry for garnish
- Ice cubes

Instructions:

Fill a shaker with ice cubes.

Add gin, maraschino liqueur, crème de violette, and fresh lemon juice to the shaker.
Shake the ingredients well to combine and chill the mixture.
Strain the mixture into a chilled martini or coupe glass.
Garnish with a maraschino cherry.

The Aviation is known for its floral and citrusy notes, with the crème de violette providing a subtle violet flavor and the maraschino liqueur adding sweetness and complexity. Adjust the proportions based on your taste preferences, as the intensity of these ingredients can vary. Enjoy this classic cocktail responsibly!

Southside

Ingredients:

- 2 oz gin
- 3/4 oz fresh lime juice
- 3/4 oz simple syrup
- 6-8 fresh mint leaves
- Mint sprig for garnish
- Ice cubes

Instructions:

In a shaker, muddle the fresh mint leaves with the simple syrup.
Add gin and fresh lime juice to the shaker.
Fill the shaker with ice cubes.
Shake the ingredients well to combine, muddle the mint, and chill the mixture.
Strain the mixture into a chilled martini or rocks glass filled with ice.
Garnish with a mint sprig.

The Southside is known for its bright and citrusy flavor with a hint of mint. It's a classic cocktail that is perfect for warm weather or any time you're in the mood for a refreshing and herbal drink. Enjoy responsibly!

Rosemary Gin Fizz

Ingredients:

- 2 oz gin
- 3/4 oz fresh lemon juice
- 1/2 oz simple syrup
- 1 sprig of fresh rosemary
- Club soda
- Rosemary sprig for garnish
- Ice cubes

Instructions:

In a shaker, muddle the fresh rosemary leaves with the simple syrup.
Add gin and fresh lemon juice to the shaker.
Fill the shaker with ice cubes.
Shake the ingredients well to combine, muddle the rosemary, and chill the mixture.
Strain the mixture into a highball glass filled with ice.
Top it up with club soda.
Gently stir to combine.
Garnish with a rosemary sprig.

The Rosemary Gin Fizz offers a wonderful blend of herbal, citrusy, and effervescent flavors. Adjust the simple syrup quantity based on your sweetness preference. Enjoy this aromatic and refreshing cocktail responsibly!

Champagne Cocktails:
Classic Champagne Cocktail

Ingredients:

- 1 sugar cube
- Angostura bitters
- Champagne or sparkling wine
- Lemon twist for garnish

Instructions:

Place a sugar cube in the bottom of a champagne flute.
Add a few dashes of Angostura bitters directly onto the sugar cube. The number of dashes can be adjusted based on your preference for bitterness.
Pour chilled champagne or sparkling wine into the glass, allowing it to dissolve the sugar cube.
Garnish with a twist of lemon by expressing the oils over the drink and dropping it into the glass.

The Classic Champagne Cocktail is known for its simplicity and the way it enhances the effervescence of the champagne with a hint of sweetness and bitterness from the sugar and bitters. It's a perfect choice for toasting on special occasions or adding a touch of glamour to any event. Enjoy responsibly!

Hugo

Ingredients:

- 2 oz Prosecco (or any sparkling wine)
- 1 oz elderflower syrup
- 10 fresh mint leaves
- Soda water
- Lime wheel or mint sprig for garnish
- Ice cubes

Instructions:

In a wine glass or a large balloon glass, muddle the fresh mint leaves with elderflower syrup.
Add ice cubes to the glass.
Pour Prosecco over the mint and elderflower mixture.
Top it up with soda water.
Gently stir to combine.
Garnish with a lime wheel or a sprig of mint.

The Hugo is known for its light and floral flavor, making it a perfect choice for warm weather or as a refreshing aperitif. Adjust the elderflower syrup quantity based on your sweetness preference. Enjoy this delightful and bubbly cocktail responsibly!

Black Velvet

Ingredients:

- 1/2 glass of champagne or sparkling wine
- 1/2 glass of stout beer (like Guinness)

Instructions:

In a champagne flute or beer glass, pour half of the glass with your preferred champagne or sparkling wine.
Carefully pour the other half of the glass with stout beer, allowing the liquids to layer.
You can adjust the proportions to your liking, aiming for a visually appealing two-tone effect.
Optionally, give the drink a gentle stir to blend the flavors slightly.

The Black Velvet is a simple yet elegant cocktail that combines the effervescence of champagne with the rich and creamy texture of stout. It's a unique and classic choice for special occasions or for those who enjoy exploring different cocktail combinations. Enjoy responsibly!

Bramble Royale

Ingredients:

- 2 oz gin
- 1 oz blackberry liqueur (such as Crème de Mûre)
- 3/4 oz simple syrup
- 3/4 oz fresh lemon juice
- Sparkling wine
- Blackberries for garnish
- Ice cubes

Instructions:

In a shaker, combine gin, blackberry liqueur, simple syrup, and fresh lemon juice.
Fill the shaker with ice cubes.
Shake the ingredients well to combine and chill the mixture.
Strain the mixture into a rocks glass filled with ice.
Top it up with sparkling wine.
Gently stir to combine.
Garnish with blackberries.

The Bramble Royale offers a wonderful blend of berry sweetness, citrusy tartness, and the effervescence of sparkling wine. Adjust the simple syrup quantity based on your sweetness preference. Enjoy this sophisticated and flavorful cocktail responsibly!

Non-Alcoholic Mocktails:
Virgin Mojito

Ingredients:

- 8-10 fresh mint leaves
- 1 tablespoon white sugar (adjust to taste)
- 1 oz fresh lime juice
- Ice cubes
- Club soda or soda water
- Lime wedge and mint sprig for garnish

Instructions:

In a glass, muddle the fresh mint leaves with sugar and fresh lime juice. Muddle gently to release the mint's flavors without tearing the leaves.
Fill the glass with ice cubes.
Top it up with club soda or soda water.
Stir gently to combine the ingredients.
Garnish with a lime wedge and a mint sprig.

The Virgin Mojito offers a crisp and citrusy flavor with the mint providing a refreshing herbal note. It's a perfect non-alcoholic option for those who enjoy the flavors of a traditional Mojito without the alcohol. Adjust the sugar quantity based on your sweetness preference. Enjoy this mocktail responsibly!

Shirley Temple

Ingredients:

- 1/2 cup ginger ale or lemon-lime soda
- 1/2 cup lemon-lime flavored carbonated beverage (such as 7UP or Sprite)
- 1 tablespoon grenadine syrup
- Maraschino cherry for garnish
- Ice cubes

Instructions:

Fill a glass with ice cubes.
Pour equal parts ginger ale or lemon-lime soda and lemon-lime flavored carbonated beverage into the glass.
Slowly pour the grenadine syrup into the glass over the back of a spoon or by drizzling it down the side of the glass. This creates a layered effect.
Garnish with a maraschino cherry.
Optionally, give the drink a gentle stir before enjoying.

The Shirley Temple is known for its sweet and fruity taste, and it's a favorite among those who prefer non-alcoholic options. It's a great choice for parties or gatherings, and you can easily adjust the ingredients to suit your taste preferences. Enjoy this classic mocktail responsibly!

Cucumber Mint Cooler

Ingredients:

- 1/2 cucumber, sliced
- 6-8 fresh mint leaves
- 1 tablespoon simple syrup (adjust to taste)
- 1 tablespoon fresh lime juice
- Sparkling water or club soda
- Ice cubes
- Cucumber slices and mint sprig for garnish

Instructions:

In a glass, muddle the cucumber slices, mint leaves, simple syrup, and fresh lime juice.
Fill the glass with ice cubes.
Top it up with sparkling water or club soda.
Stir gently to combine the ingredients.
Garnish with cucumber slices and a mint sprig.

The Cucumber Mint Cooler offers a cool and herbaceous flavor, making it a perfect choice for hot days or as a refreshing alternative. Adjust the simple syrup quantity based on your sweetness preference. Enjoy this hydrating cooler responsibly!

Berry Sparkler

Ingredients:

- 1/2 cup mixed berries (such as strawberries, blueberries, raspberries)
- 1 tablespoon simple syrup
- 1 tablespoon fresh lemon juice
- Sparkling water or club soda
- Ice cubes
- Mint sprig for garnish

Instructions:

In a glass, muddle the mixed berries with simple syrup and fresh lemon juice.
Fill the glass with ice cubes.
Top it up with sparkling water or club soda.
Stir gently to combine the ingredients.
Garnish with a mint sprig.

Feel free to customize the Berry Sparkler with your favorite combination of berries. Adjust the simple syrup quantity based on your sweetness preference. This drink offers a burst of fruity flavors and effervescence, making it a fantastic non-alcoholic option for any occasion. Enjoy responsibly!

Seasonal and Holiday Cocktails:

Apple Cider Bourbon Smash

Ingredients:

- 2 oz bourbon
- 4 oz apple cider
- 1/2 oz fresh lemon juice
- 1/2 oz simple syrup (adjust to taste)
- Apple slices for garnish
- Cinnamon stick for garnish
- Ice cubes

Instructions:

In a shaker, combine bourbon, apple cider, fresh lemon juice, and simple syrup.
Fill the shaker with ice cubes.
Shake the ingredients well to combine and chill the mixture.
Strain the mixture into a glass filled with ice.
Garnish with apple slices and a cinnamon stick.

The Apple Cider Bourbon Smash offers a perfect blend of the smoky notes from bourbon, the sweetness of apple cider, and the tartness of fresh lemon juice. Adjust the simple syrup quantity based on your sweetness preference. It's a wonderful cocktail for fall or winter, capturing the essence of seasonal flavors. Enjoy responsibly!

Cranberry Orange Mimosa

Ingredients:

- 2 oz cranberry juice (unsweetened)
- 1 oz orange juice
- 4 oz chilled sparkling wine or champagne
- Orange twist for garnish
- Fresh cranberries for garnish (optional)

- Ice cubes (optional)

Instructions:

In a champagne flute, pour cranberry juice.
Add orange juice to the glass.
Top it up with chilled sparkling wine or champagne.
Optionally, add ice cubes to the glass.
Gently stir to combine the juices and sparkling wine.
Garnish with an orange twist and fresh cranberries if desired.

The Cranberry Orange Mimosa combines the tartness of cranberry juice with the citrusy sweetness of orange juice, creating a vibrant and festive drink. Adjust the proportions based on your taste preferences. Enjoy this delightful and bubbly cocktail responsibly!

Pumpkin Spice White Russian

Ingredients:

- 2 oz vodka
- 1 oz coffee liqueur (such as Kahlúa)
- 1 oz pumpkin spice creamer or pumpkin spice syrup
- Ice cubes
- Ground cinnamon or nutmeg for garnish (optional)

Instructions:

Fill a rocks glass with ice cubes.
Pour vodka and coffee liqueur over the ice.
Add the pumpkin spice creamer or pumpkin spice syrup to the glass.
Stir gently to combine the ingredients.
Optionally, sprinkle ground cinnamon or nutmeg on top for extra flavor and garnish.

The Pumpkin Spice White Russian offers a delightful blend of coffee, vodka, and the cozy flavors of pumpkin spice. Adjust the pumpkin spice creamer or syrup quantity based on your preference for sweetness and spiciness. It's a perfect cocktail for fall and holiday gatherings, bringing a touch of seasonal warmth to your glass. Enjoy responsibly!

Eggnog Martini

Ingredients:

- 2 oz vanilla vodka
- 2 oz eggnog
- 1/2 oz simple syrup (optional, to taste)
- Ice cubes
- Ground nutmeg for garnish

Instructions:

In a shaker, combine vanilla vodka, eggnog, and simple syrup if desired.
Fill the shaker with ice cubes.
Shake the ingredients well to combine and chill the mixture.
Strain the mixture into a chilled martini glass.
Garnish with a sprinkle of ground nutmeg.

The Eggnog Martini offers a decadent blend of vanilla, eggnog, and a hint of sweetness. Adjust the simple syrup quantity based on your sweetness preference. It's a perfect cocktail for holiday celebrations or cozy evenings by the fireplace. Enjoy this festive and creamy martini responsibly!

Herb and Fruit Infusions:
Infused Berry Vodka

Ingredients:

- 1 cup mixed berries (strawberries, blueberries, raspberries, blackberries, etc.)
- 1 bottle (750 ml) vodka
- 2-3 tablespoons granulated sugar (optional, to taste)

Instructions:

Wash the berries thoroughly and remove any stems.
In a clean glass jar or bottle with a tight-sealing lid, add the mixed berries.
If you prefer a slightly sweeter infusion, you can add granulated sugar to the berries.
Pour the vodka over the berries, ensuring that they are fully submerged.
Seal the jar or bottle tightly and shake gently to combine the ingredients.
Place the infused vodka in a cool, dark place for at least a few days to allow the flavors to meld. You can leave it for up to a week for a more intense infusion.
After the desired infusion time, strain the vodka through a fine mesh strainer or cheesecloth into a clean bottle or jar, discarding the used berries.
If needed, you can filter the vodka a second time through a coffee filter for extra clarity.
Store the infused berry vodka in the refrigerator for freshness.

Now you have a vibrant and flavorful berry-infused vodka that you can use in various cocktails or simply enjoy over ice. Get creative with your infused vodka by trying different berry combinations or experimenting with additional herbs and spices!

Citrus Basil Gin

Ingredients:

- 2 oz gin
- 1/2 oz fresh lime juice
- 1/2 oz fresh lemon juice
- 1 oz simple syrup
- 4-6 fresh basil leaves
- Citrus slices or twists for garnish
- Ice cubes

Instructions:

In a shaker, muddle the fresh basil leaves with simple syrup.
Add gin, fresh lime juice, and fresh lemon juice to the shaker.
Fill the shaker with ice cubes.
Shake the ingredients well to combine, muddle the basil, and chill the mixture.
Strain the mixture into a glass filled with ice.
Garnish with citrus slices or twists.

The Citrus Basil Gin cocktail offers a delightful balance of citrusy brightness and herbal freshness from the basil. Adjust the simple syrup quantity based on your sweetness preference. It's a perfect choice for warm weather or any time you're in the mood for a vibrant and aromatic drink. Enjoy responsibly!

Cucumber Mint Tequila

Ingredients:

- 2 oz tequila
- 1/2 oz triple sec (orange liqueur)
- 1 oz fresh lime juice
- 1/2 oz simple syrup (adjust to taste)
- 4-6 cucumber slices
- 8-10 fresh mint leaves
- Ice cubes
- Cucumber wheel and mint sprig for garnish

Instructions:

In a shaker, muddle the cucumber slices and fresh mint leaves with simple syrup.
Add tequila, triple sec, and fresh lime juice to the shaker.
Fill the shaker with ice cubes.
Shake the ingredients well to combine, muddle the cucumber and mint, and chill the mixture.
Strain the mixture into a glass filled with ice.
Garnish with a cucumber wheel and a mint sprig.

This Cucumber Mint Tequila cocktail offers a crisp and herbaceous flavor profile, perfect for warm days or when you're in the mood for a refreshing drink. Adjust the simple syrup quantity based on your sweetness preference. Enjoy this delightful and cooling tequila cocktail responsibly!

Rosemary Infused Bourbon

Ingredients:

- 1 cup bourbon
- 2-3 fresh rosemary sprigs

Instructions:

Wash the rosemary sprigs and pat them dry.
In a clean glass jar or bottle with a tight-sealing lid, place the rosemary sprigs.
Pour the bourbon over the rosemary, ensuring that the sprigs are fully submerged.
Seal the jar or bottle tightly and give it a gentle shake to combine.
Place the rosemary-infused bourbon in a cool, dark place for at least 24 hours to allow the flavors to meld. You can leave it longer for a more intense infusion, up to a few days.
After the desired infusion time, strain the bourbon through a fine mesh strainer or cheesecloth into a clean bottle or jar, removing the used rosemary.
If needed, you can filter the bourbon a second time through a coffee filter for extra clarity.
Store the rosemary-infused bourbon in a cool, dark place.

Now you have a unique rosemary-infused bourbon that can be used in various cocktails. Try it in classic bourbon-based drinks or experiment with creating your own signature cocktails. Enjoy responsibly!

Coffee and Dessert Cocktails:
White Russian

Ingredients:

- 2 oz vodka
- 1 oz coffee liqueur (such as Kahlúa)
- 1 oz heavy cream or milk
- Ice cubes

Instructions:

Fill a rocks glass with ice cubes.
Pour vodka and coffee liqueur over the ice.
Add heavy cream or milk to the glass.
Stir gently to combine the ingredients.

The White Russian is known for its smooth and rich flavor, with the coffee liqueur providing a hint of sweetness and the cream adding a creamy texture. Adjust the proportions based on your taste preferences, and you can also experiment with flavored vodkas or different coffee liqueurs to create variations. Enjoy this classic cocktail responsibly!

Chocolate Martini

Ingredients:

- 2 oz chocolate liqueur (such as crème de cacao)
- 2 oz vodka
- 1 oz cream or half-and-half
- Chocolate syrup for garnish
- Chocolate shavings or cocoa powder for garnish (optional)
- Ice cubes

Instructions:

Drizzle chocolate syrup inside a chilled martini glass, creating a decorative pattern if desired.
In a shaker, combine chocolate liqueur, vodka, and cream.
Fill the shaker with ice cubes.
Shake the ingredients well to combine and chill the mixture.
Strain the mixture into the prepared martini glass.
Optionally, garnish with chocolate shavings or a dusting of cocoa powder on top.

The Chocolate Martini offers a luxurious and velvety chocolate flavor with a hint of vodka. Adjust the proportions based on your sweetness preference, and feel free to experiment with different chocolate liqueurs for variations. It's a perfect dessert cocktail for chocolate lovers. Enjoy responsibly!